William Davidson Institute
AT THE UNIVERSITY OF MICHIGAN

MICHIGAN
ROSS SCHOOL OF BUSINESS

AF879694

case 1-428-915
January 21, 2010

ITC e-Choupal 3.0

ITC is one of India's largest private sector conglomerate with diversified presence in industries including, food, agriculture, hotels, cigarettes, personal care, paper and stationery, and a market capitalization of US $19 Billion and 2008 sales exceeding $5 Billion. ITC is ranked among world's most reputed companies by Forbes magazine and listed as one of India's most valuable companies by local Indian business magazines. The Agri-Business at ITC is one of India's largest exporters of agricultural products. ITC's e-Choupal initiative that enables rural Indian farmers to enhance their efficiency through price transparency over the Internet had received accolades internationally.

In the summer of 2008, executives of ITC gathered together to discuss the next iteration of their successful initiative, e-Choupal. ITC had first created e-Choupals, or internet-enabled computer stations based in villages to provide information on weather, best practices, crop details, market prices, and important local news to farmers in 1999. That early project expanded to a version 2.0 between 2003 and 2008, and after years of the 2.0 model, the team was beginning to sense that an updated version, encompassing what they had learned through the initial years, would be necessary to further encourage and foster the entrepreneurial spirit of the farmers and rural communities.

As S. Sivakumar, CEO of ITC's Agribusiness Division, and his team began to envision the e-Choupal 3.0 model, they reflected on how far they had come since the inception of e-Choupal in 1999, a journey depicted in **Figure 1**. Beginning with the idea that each farmer is a micro-producer, the 1.0 model focused on a one-way supply chain from the farmers to ITC, with ITC purchasing soya and other commodities from rural communities. The 2.0 e-Choupal expanded on this concept and incorporated the idea that farmers are also micro-consumers. To serve these consumers, ITC expanded its supply chain to include selling consumer-packaged goods to the farming communities. The team now reached a conclusion that the time had come for the 2.0 model to be augmented in order to accommodate the changes that had occurred. Through the support of the e-Choupal, farmers had also become entrepreneurs, requiring a deeper personalization of the approach and facilitation of greater economic opportunities for members of the community.

Throughout, ITC's e-Choupal initiative ensured a continuing focus on a positive social impact, as shown in **Figure 2**. A tenet of 1.0 was treating farmers with dignity and respect. All commercial transactions between ITC and the farmers were transparent and fair, which stood in a stark contrast to the *mandi* (a marketplace in rural India). E-Choupal 2.0's shift to a two-way supply chain gave farmers and rural communities access to consumer goods that were previously unavailable, and 3.0 would expand this access to provide more customized offerings based on local demand. Positive social impact was central to ITC's work and would continue to be a core aspect of e-Choupal 3.0.

Katharine Egan, Annie Kneedler, Pradeep Sagi, and Harveen Sethi prepared this case under the supervision of University of Michigan Ross School of Business Professors CK Prahalad and MS Krishnan. ©2010, The William Davidson Institute

Figure 1

ITC e-Choupal Timeline

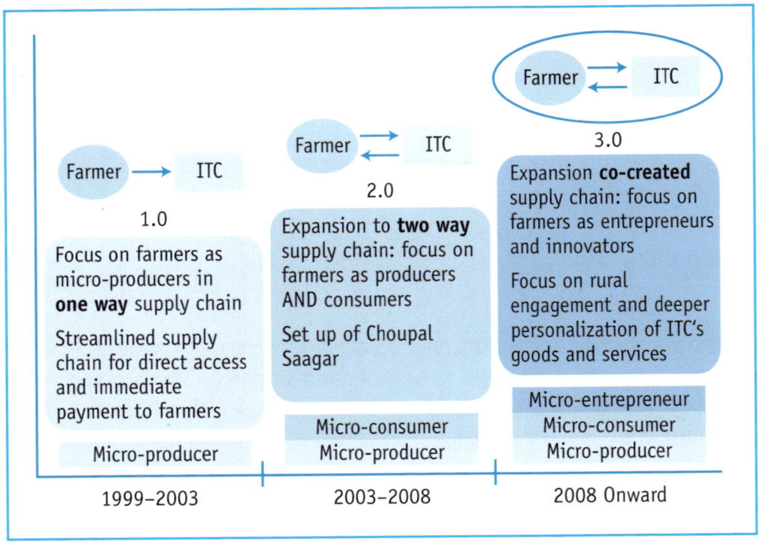

Figure 2

e-Choupal Social Impact Timeline

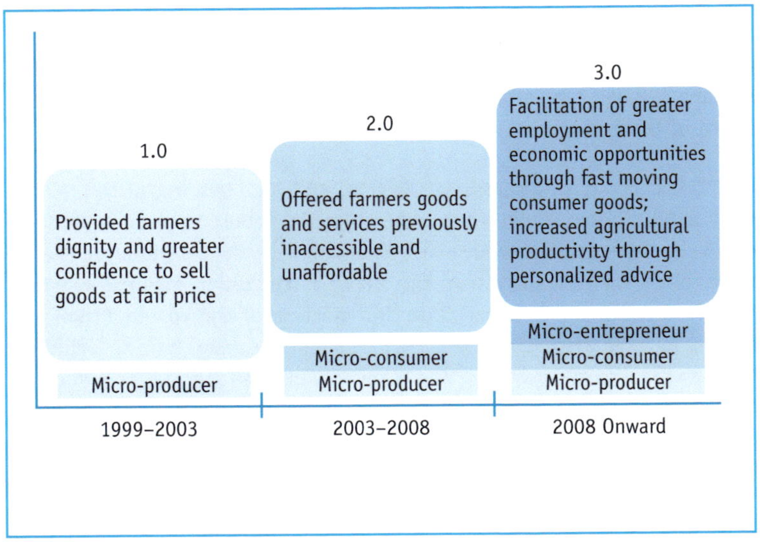

This case provides a synopsis of the 1.0 and 2.0 e-Choupal models as well as a detailed overview of what was planned for the 3.0 e-Choupal. It concludes at a juncture when the model is yet to be fully executed by ITC, allowing the reader to debate ITC's strategic approach.

ITC

ITC innovatively used information and communication technologies to establish an information and business platform for India's small and poor farmers, who were hitherto operating in unorganized traditional markets that exploited the disadvantaged position of farmers. Since its first initiative to set up Internet kiosk-based e-Choupals, ITC has pioneered rural commercial engagement, demonstrating the power and impact of coordinating partnerships across public, private, and not-for-profit sectors in connecting rural India to urban markets.

ITC e-Choupal 1.0

The first version of e-Choupal was a response to the inefficient and ineffective agriculture supply chain that constituted the majority of ITC's agricultural export business.[1] Faced with the challenge of providing new solutions to transform ineffective traditional practices and also enhance the effectiveness of ITC's International Business Division, S. Sivakumar proposed a pioneering use of digital technologies to improve the agriculture supply chain.

The key issue that put farmers at a significant disadvantage, and one that the local market *mandis* exploited fully, was the lack of information on the reasonable price that their crops could command. The *mandi* system was characterized by corruption and ineffectiveness and the *mandis* acted as the only delivery point where farmers could bring their produce for sale to traders (**Figure 3**). Farmers in isolated villages were exploited because they lacked knowledge on what price they could reasonably command for their crops. Lacking resources to analyze or anticipate price trends, farmers relied on local information within a village to decide when to sell and which *mandi* to use. Having already harvested their crops and lacking alternative markets, farmers were forced to accept the price offered when they arrived at the *mandi* as they had no bargaining power with the agents.

Figure 3
Old Process

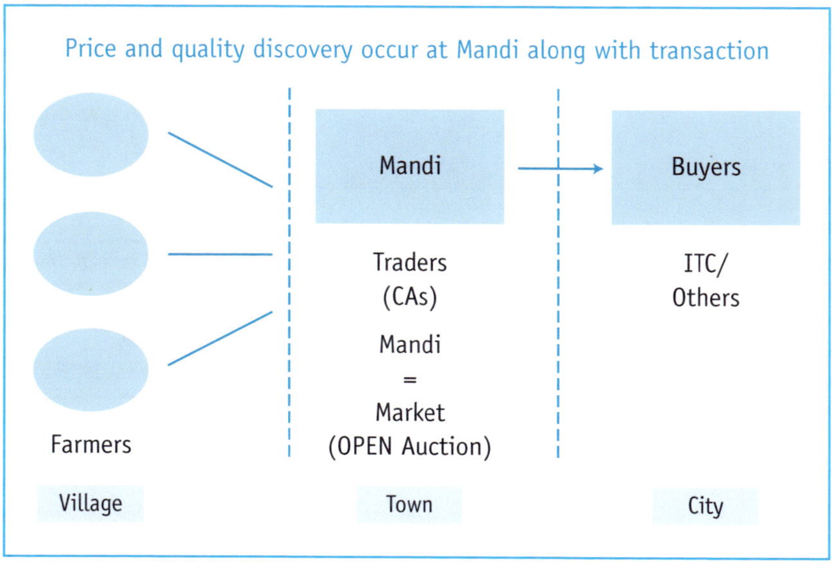

ITC created the e-Choupal program to benefit farmers first by addressing this information asymmetry. Building on the concept of *choupal* (meaning a meeting place in Hindi), ITC installed computers with Internet connections in villages to provide information on weather, best practices, crop details, market prices, important local news, and an interactive question and answer forum. This digital infrastructure created an e-Choupal, a virtual meeting place that provided transparent access to information that was previously unavailable at the village level. The original e-Choupal was housed in a Sanchalak's house,* and he was seen as the key connection between ITC and the village. ITC built on the inherent trust and respect extended to the Sanchalaks to assimilate with the local community.

Concurrently, ITC convinced the government to allow agricultural transactions to take place outside the *mandi*, which was previously prohibited by the Agricultural Produce Marketing Act. Avoiding transportation to the *mandi*, the farmer now had the opportunity to take a sample of his produce to the e-Choupal and have the Sanchalak inspect it to get a benchmark price based on the quality. Open markets allowed ITC to set up its own hubs as marketplaces for farmers to sell produce based on their knowledge of fair market prices. Unlike the *mandi*, the hubs had a transparent and non-wasteful process for inspections, weighing, and payments. ITC paid farmers immediately for their produce, and reimbursed them for the cost of transportation. A key tenet of ITC's approach was freedom of choice for farmers. Empowered with market information, farmers could now choose to sell to ITC or the *mandi*, depending on where they would get a better deal. The model of 1.0 is best illustrated in **Figure 4**.

Figure 4

e-Choupal Supply Chain

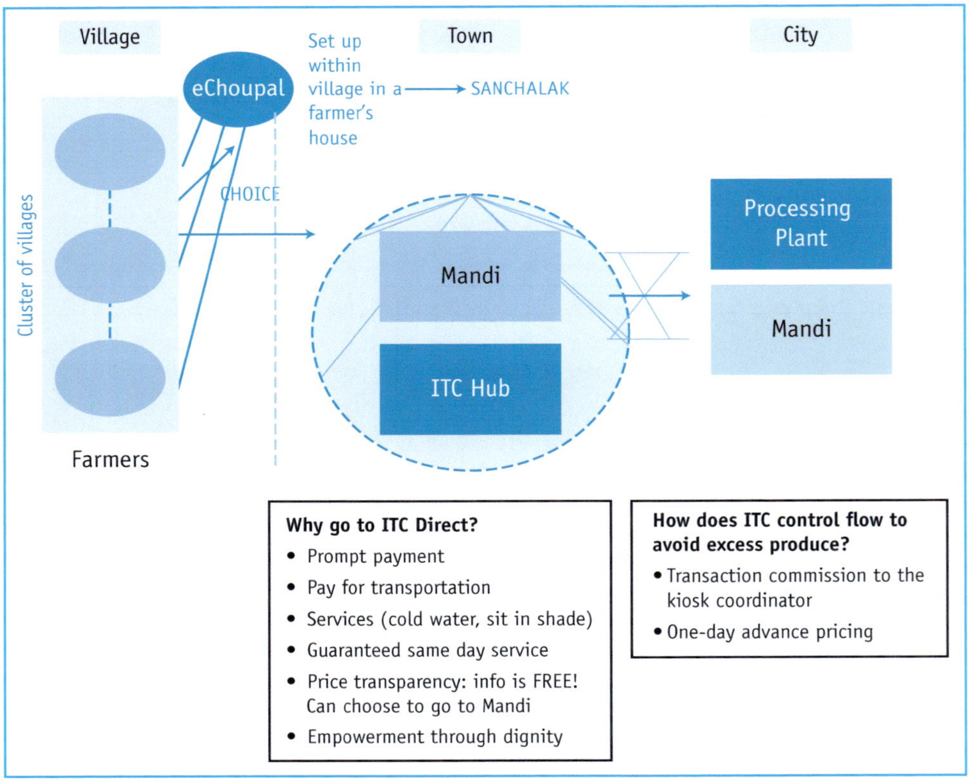

*The Sanchalak is the ITC representative in a village. The computer is in the Sanchalak's house, and he also has equipment to test the quality of crops.

The e-Choupal platform empowered the community through real-time information and customized knowledge, and facilitated the development of a community-responsive grassroots organization built on freedom of choice and local management with self-interest. It also ensured efficiency through competition, overcame the challenges of rural landscape through virtual aggregation, giving it the power of scale, and delivered the benefits of specialization through collaboration. In the process, ITC put in place a "virtuous cycle" created by larger incomes and founded on trust to capture the latent value in the dormant markets of the economy in rural India. Above all, the platform approach of e-Choupal was proven scalable (more than 6500 e-Choupals have been setup to serve approximately 4 million farmers), giving a multiplier effect on the economic and social benefits.[2]

With e-Choupal 1.0, in addition to the positive social impact of improving farmers' confidence and sense of social dignity, the overall economic benefits to the farmer included better access to information, and better timing of information to aid in fetching an optimal price for produce; shorter transaction duration; greater weighing accuracy and honest payments; and reimbursement of costs. ITC benefited from the program through savings from the streamlined supply chain, reliable access to goods, and reduced freight costs. Most important, ITC had greater control of quality, and was able to better manage risk by developing long-term supplier relationships with farmers. The relationship of trust built up through this process was the key driver for ITC's further commercial engagement in rural India.

While e-Choupal 1.0 certainly brought benefits to ITC and the rural farmers, the organization also realized that it was not sufficient to capture value across the entire network. ITC had built the network connecting the farmers to each other and ITC via the Sanchalak and had created trust in the community. It was able to directly communicate with the farmers, minimizing the intermediary merchant power and opening an opportunity for ITC to expand. However, the e-Choupal 1.0 model met only part of the demands and opportunity created by the cultivated relationship that ITC had built with farmers. While the e-Choupal initiative provided the community with an avenue to receive fair pricing on commodities, there were gaps in value capture as the money that the farmers were receiving was being spent at stores, merchants, and goods in the area outside ITC's reach.

ITC e-Choupal 2.0

After the tremendous success of launching the e-Choupal project, ITC realized that a significant opportunity had emerged to expand the model to engage in a two-way channel to truly connect farmers to local and global markets from both a production and consumption point of view. Recognizing the farmers' needs for agricultural inputs (fertilizers, agrichemicals, seeds) as well as credit and insurance, ITC saw an opportunity to make these products available to the same communities that were selling their produce to ITC, thereby viewing marketing and distribution to India's population living in rural areas as a potential growth engine.[3]

ITC built on the 1.0 model in the form of storefronts called Choupal Saagars. These Saagars were situated at the center of a cluster of approximately 40 e-Choupals, and offered a range of services. Essentially a Saagar served as a marketing platform and storefront for agri-equipment, personal consumption products, insurance, health services (including telemedicine), an agri-extension clinic, a fuel station, and a food court. When a farmer came to the Choupal Saagar to sell his crop, his grain was weighed and then he was handed a payment slip that he redeemed by going inside the Choupal Saagar. This drove the farmer into the store and exposed him to the various products and services available at the Saagar.

With the establishment of e-Choupal 2.0, farmers could now order high-quality agricultural inputs and consumer goods through the Sanchalak or directly through the Saagar. In this regard, the farmer became both ITC's supplier and consumer. With the rural network established, ITC was able to provide agricultural inputs and fast moving consumer goods (FMCG) products to farmers through the Sanchalaks. ITC relied on the trust-based relationship established with the Sanchalaks to facilitate transactions of insurance and for distribution of goods ordered. Sanchalaks stocked fertilizers, pesticides, gas lanterns, and household goods to sell to the villages. A Samyojak oversaw a region of Sanchalaks, managing the inventory of goods and serving as the link between Sanchalaks and ITC headquarters.

Through its efforts, ITC realized that by facilitating empowered access to the markets, private businesses could build a profitable business model out of streamlining the rural value chains. This also facilitated the creation of market infrastructure not only for the farmers, but also for the company, in enabling sales of a host of products and services to these traditionally under-served consumers.[4]

By progressively linking the digital infrastructure to a physical network of rural business hubs and agricultural extension services, ITC transformed the way farmers did business, and the way rural markets worked. The e-Choupal Saagar hub and spoke combination transformed rural communities to a new level of productivity and consumption. The services at the e-Choupals helped farmers improve productivity and crop yields, and the Choupal Saagars provided the rural communities with a one-stop shopping experience comparable to urban levels.

Despite what had been accomplished so far, many challenges remained to develop e-Choupal as a significant two-way multidimensional delivery channel that efficiently facilitated the flow of goods and services to and from largely inaccessible rural markets. Rural distribution was becoming complex due to the numerous interactions between the partner companies, their distributors and the Samyojaks, and ITC did not have much control over the transactions.

The rural distribution of various products and services such as fast moving consumer goods, agri-inputs, and financial services had varying economic structures, logistics, and profitability. The company learned that many Sanchalaks were losing interest in the role and felt that they were wasting time and effort in developing these businesses without much return. There was also a huge capacity challenge as the Sanchalaks lacked the business skills and entrepreneurial abilities to engage in both farming and other entrepreneurial activities such as selling, offering credit and inventory management. The company realized that there was a need to train the retailers in merchandising and working capital management for the goods distribution to be effective. ITC also felt the need to engage in a deeper understanding of the unique requirements of retailers and their customers, because the information and insights were not properly captured at the rural level and transmitted to ITC.

ITC e-Choupal 3.0

Based on the points of success and challenges resulting from the implementation of e-Choupal 1.0 and 2.0, ITC continued to reflect and evolve its thinking for the next phase. Deeper rural engagement through the e-Choupal initiative enabled ITC to recognize even greater opportunities for co-creation with farmers in developing new anchor businesses and creating deeper personalization. ITC's efforts to date had allowed it to understand the uniqueness of the farmers—both as micro-producers and micro-consumers. As a result, ITC improved its knowledge of the environment and the farmers—building the platform for 3.0. The vision of e-Choupal 3.0 was to build upon past efforts and co-create with farmers, thus empowering farmers to be micro-entrepreneurs and micro-innovators.

ITC employed a similar process for shaping 3.0 as it did for 2.0. It invested significant time and resources in evaluating the lessons learned from 2.0, studying the challenges faced and discovering opportunities in the process of working with farmers as producers and consumers respectively. E-Choupal 2.0 revealed significant opportunities for a new ITC platform to fuel greater growth for ITC, and with it, to continue to achieve still greater social benefits for the villages where ITC operated. Based on this evaluation of learning, ITC recognized the need and opportunity to create personalized solutions to foster interaction and co-creation among participants. As such, ITC decided to leverage its existing technology and social architecture in order to build a platform based on new anchor businesses and deeper personalization. These two main concepts were the key drivers behind e-Choupal 3.0.

Approach and Methodology

Focused on co-creating with farmers and harnessing their entrepreneurship, ITC envisioned developing the 3.0 platform to encompass service, product, knowledge, and convenience. ITC partnered with Erehwon Innovation Consulting, a consulting firm focused on designing innovative business models, to seek fundamental insights and to develop a model based on solutions that would be scalable throughout rural India. Accordingly, the team used the methodology of "Insight Search Dialogue" (**Figure 5**) to shape the 3.0 platform. Upon designing a sustainable business model, ITC planned to prototype and version the idea from conception to scale in order to learn from the strengths and weaknesses of pilot programs, and accordingly adapt the plan of execution for the broad rollout of the 3.0 platform to millions of farmers across India.

Figure 5

Insight Process Phases

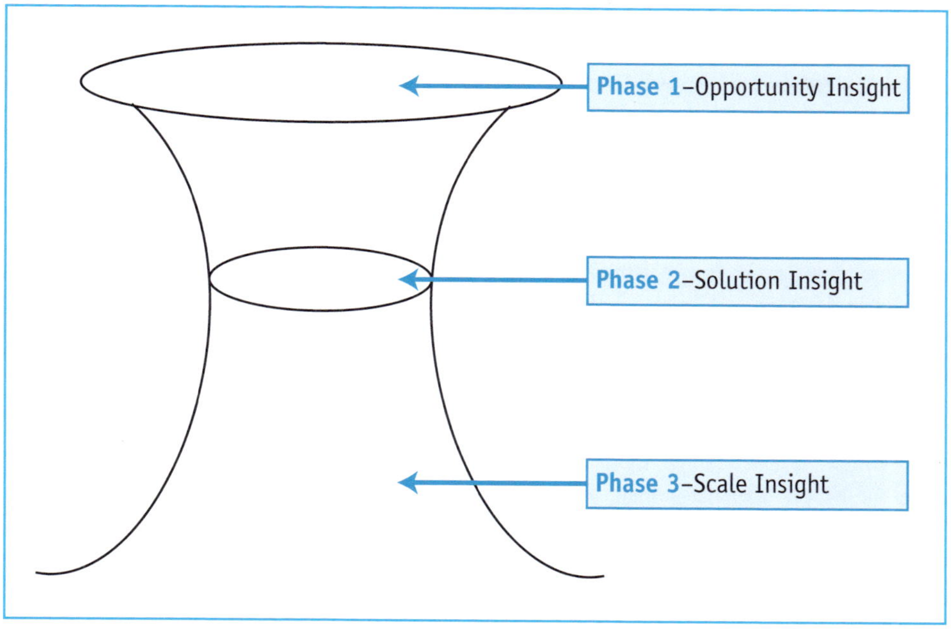

One of the important findings that emerged was that some entrepreneurial Sanchalaks and farmer communities had been able to deploy the power of the e-Choupal channel to realize better results. This was an opportunity—could a personalized approach help create more such entrepreneurs? Addressing this need for personalization would require a shift in the channel's existing paradigm, from pushing output to pulling (or proactively facilitating and enabling) output.

The primary assumption was that farmers were the experts and knew the products and skills needed, and the economic benefits could shape the demand. ITC wanted to create a supply chain embedded with trust, incorporating many partners and broadly reaching out to the target recipients. ITC had built a strong relationship with vendors and partners, but the specific value propositions needed to be identified and leveraged. In order to do so, the value proposition for each partner had to be made clear as ITC leveraged its relationships in rural India and connected the partners to them. This could be done through numerous ways, whether via live demonstrations of products in the field, training partners, or bundling products and services together. The vision was to provide a large audience for companies to develop new relationships and for farmers to benefit from new techniques and technologies.

ITC played a role at the center of the hub, filtering the partner companies and ensuring that the farmers were given a choice. It wanted to be perceived as a platform enabler providing information and choice. ITC's strategy was to foster an ecosystem in order to create rich partners and commitment for its e-Choupal 3.0 model.

ITC wanted to understand some of the greatest challenges in these communities and therefore it sent thirty-five employees from across functions to travel the span of India for four months to gather insights. These insights led to brainstorming, synthesizing, and developing pilot programs across India to determine what methods would best meet the challenges identified in e-Choupal 2.0. In the solution insight search phase, ITC was challenged to create a solution for all of the identified challenges, creating prototypes within a realistic target budget. Unlike a usual pilot program designed to validate the efficacy of an idea, this approach helped ITC initiate a few focused experiments designed to find solution insights in areas where new learning was needed for acceptability and scale.

The top leadership team of ITC's agri-business division traversed rural India and identified potential areas of opportunity to develop relationships with farmers and villages, and further integrate ITC process with its constituents. Thereafter four task forces consisting of cross-functional strengths were created to focus on specific innovation-sensitive areas. The overarching themes that guided these task forces concentrated on co-creation of new anchor businesses and personalized solutions for farmers, complemented with micro-entrepreneurship.

The insights identified through the task forces led ITC to the scale phase of the process, where the pilot programs were re-evaluated and adjusted and then rolled out on a larger scale across many e-Choupals. The prototypes were designed as a series of experiments that were improved over time. Each version led to new learning that was integrated into the next version of the experiment. This allowed for tremendous learning on the ground—and a dynamic model of evolution of the idea as it was versioned.

Business Model

Insights-based research led ITC to identify the need for new anchor businesses to diversify and stabilize ITC in the future. ITC also determined that personalization should play a key role in customizing the experience for each farmer and optimizing the relationship between rural India and ITC. Using these two fundamental concepts as well as the insights identified through the task forces, ITC created a new way for farmers to customize their learning and co-create their experiences through access to resources and opportunities in ITC's ecosystem of partners and knowledge base.

ITC's e-Choupal 3.0 model illustrated in **Figure 6** had two key drivers of the three new businesses of 3.0, all of which were supported by three key enablers. The key drivers were deeper personalization and new anchor businesses. These were the drivers behind the new businesses described in following sections: FMCG, Agri-inputs and Demonstration Farms, and Rural Employment Exchange. All of these businesses, or the pillars of the business, were supported by the enablers, or the foundation, of the business model. These enablers—technology, convergence, and social architecture—were the foundation of the co-creation experience platform.

Figure 6
e-Choupal 3.0 Business Model

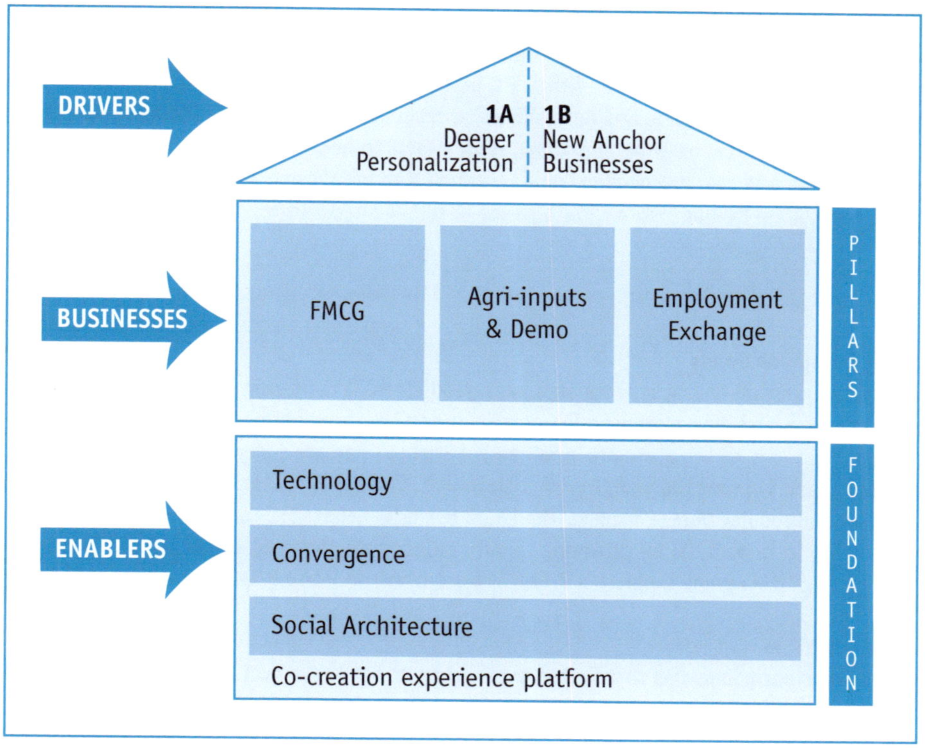

ITC e-Choupal 3.0 Drivers

Deeper Personalization

There were two tenets of deeper personalization. The first was to gain a deeper level of communication with individual farmers in order to respond to their needs in a more customized manner. Traditionally, the link to farmers had been through a lead farmer of the village—the Sanchalak—who intermediated transactions between ITC and farmers. While the information ITC received at an aggregate level from each Sanchalak had been adequate to date, there was one gap: The overall ITC network could not capture the information, requests, or feedback that the farmers provided the Sanchalaks. The deeper personalization platform of 3.0 was intended to capture this information from farmers directly. While intermediation by the Sanchalak would continue to exist, ITC intended to leverage mobile technology to supplement these interactions to further personalize solutions for farmers.

The second key tenet was to support e-Choupal scalability. Personalization had occurred informally. Interaction between farmers and ITC had been intermittent. As ITC continued to expand across the country, it was constrained in resources to interact with farmers individually and provide personalized advice informally. Thus deeper personalization was intended, to transform the informal interaction of personalized advice to a more structured method of providing advice through technology. This was intended to create a virtuous cycle of personalization, wherein farmers sent information through mobile technology about any issues they faced, and received personalized advice. Additionally, ITC could then use this information to create a base for data analytics, which it could aggregate to develop (internally or through a partnership) more personalized solutions.

New Anchor Businesses

The second driver of ITC's e-Choupal 3.0 strategy was developing new anchor businesses to diversify ITC's portfolio. As a result of the high inflation in 2006, India's growth trajectory slowed significantly, prices increased and agricultural production suffered. At the same time, the Indian government slowed down reform activities, particularly through the Essential Commodities Act, which controlled stock levels and stopped derivative pricing in commodities. ITC began to rethink its model, which relied on commodity sourcing, and explored new models and possibilities to scale and expand. In addition to the above factors, the ITC food businesses were reaching a plateau, with a limit to how much additional FMCG products could be branded and sold, and how much value could be added through these activities. With all of these factors in mind, ITC focused on finding new anchor businesses outside agriculture.

ITC e-Choupal 3.0 Businesses

Fast Moving Consumer Goods

The rural distribution of fast moving consumer goods (FMCG) started in 2003 with the introduction of ITC branded products and the program scaled quickly due to the introduction of a portfolio of products from partner companies. This direct access to rural markets helped partner companies increase the availability of their products and improve the visibility of their brands. The Sanchalak and the Samyojak benefited from increased sales and regular flow of income. The FMCG business helped ITC to realize its vision of improving the quality of life in rural India by providing quality products to the rural communities. There was also a strong synergy with the parent company's vision of becoming the leading FMCG company in India.

Original Business Model

Originally, partner companies distributed their products to the Samyojak. The Samyojak supplied the products to the Sanchalak, who in turn distributed to the retailers. This was a complex supply chain with multiple sources of supply for the Samyojak, who had to interact with many partner companies on a daily basis for products, logistics, and cash management. ITC did not have control over the transactions between the partner companies and their distributors, and it had a low visibility on the interactions between the Samyojak and the distributors.

The Sanchalak was expected to purchase stocks from the Samyojak and subsequently transact with retailers. There was an informal exchange between the Sanchalak and the retailer. The Sanchalak had the contextual knowledge; he knew the retailers and understood what they bought and what products sold well. He also had insights on consumers' behavior in terms of their needs and requirements. A lot of information was exchanged among the Sanchalak, the retailers, and the consumers; knowledge was captured, and there was a certain value generated in the process. However, these deep insights rested with the Sanchalaks, some of whom engaged with the retailers and consumers, while others did not.

To design a new model, ITC studied the high-performing and under-performing Sanchalaks to understand their success factors and limitations. There was a hesitation on the part of many Sanchalaks to be in the business of distributing FMCG, because they were predominantly farmers with no distribution capabilities. In addition, it was difficult for many of them to build skills such as selling, credit management, and inventory management. As the FMCG business was a low-margin, high-volume business, it was essential to have high inventory turns and robust money management. So, it was decided to take the Sanchalak out of the direct purchasing and distribution process and allow him to be involved in the areas where he could excel most.

New Engagement Model

The proposed model was an engagement model, where ITC would buy the products from the partner companies and have a central distribution center to distribute the products to the Samyojak, who supplied directly to the retailer. The motivation behind this new model was to offer a personalized value proposition for the retailer by moving away from an informal exchange among the retailer, Sanchalak, Samyojak, partner companies, and ITC to a more streamlined exchange. ITC recognized that information technology would be the backbone to deliver the value proposition, enable personalization, and offer smart exchange at affordable prices. A streamlined and digitally enabled supply chain would ensure better efficiencies and economies of scale in the transactions with the partner companies. ITC would also have higher control and visibility on transactions to enable smart decision-making.

ITC planned to leverage the Sanchalaks' strengths by keeping them involved in aspects such as credit assessment, introducing retailers to Samyojaks, and communicating promotional schemes to the people. The Sanchalak would become a facilitator. Most Sanchalaks did not want to be seen as people just selling products and collecting money. Under the new model, the Sanchalak would not experience social alienation within the village. He would be an advocate of the value proposition and learning, empowering him. He understood the retailers and knew which retailers could be given credit based on their ability to repay and the risks associated with it. ITC intended to explore the possibility of financing the retailers by partnering with banks and making use of the Sanchalak to assess the risk to extend credit.

In a market that was characterized by scarcity of options for rural retailers, ITC planned to engage the retailers and co-create value for the rural communities. Retailers would have an opportunity to connect directly with ITC through a loyalty program and link up to a transparent and flexible system without creating a hierarchy in the system. Unlike the retailers in urban areas, who could get training from salespersons of FMCG firms, rural retailers were not trained in ordering, displaying merchandise, educating consumers, or promoting products. Most companies did not go directly to the retailers in rural India, but ITC could offer a complete portfolio of FMCG available at the retailer's doorstep. The company could also offer merchandising solutions and working capital solutions.

In the past, it was extremely difficult to get the data and information from retailers and consumers. Knowledge of the market or the consumer insights were not being captured by ITC or the partner companies. For 3.0, ITC planned to capture the value through the informal exchange between the Sanchalaks and the retailers by using technology and creating a smart exchange. This would enable smart decision-making to create new products suitable to the consumer. ITC was also looking at new mobile technologies that could enable the retailer to directly order from the Samyojak or the distribution center and to make mobile payments. This would help ITC to personalize the service to the retailers and provide an opportunity to partner companies that were leveraging this channel to connect to the retailers and the consumers.

Agri-inputs and Demonstration Farms

Even with productivity gains, farmers were still having a hard time making ends meet. To move farmers from subsistence to profit-earning and improve their standard of living, ITC needed to introduce new production techniques and higher-value crops. ITC wanted to ensure that farmers could at least earn the minimum wage, to encourage people to continue to farm rather than go to cities in search of minimum wage work. ITC had success with its CPK model in other regions, but found that it was too prescriptive, telling farmers exactly what to do rather than providing various techniques for them to choose from. As ITC was moving toward a new model, it wanted to personalize the CPK model through demonstration farms. The demonstration farms would also provide a more personalized venue for information to flow from the farmers to ITC, and vice versa. With the current CPK model, a lot of innovations from farmers were not captured and disseminated to a wider audience. With closer connections between ITC and farmers, these innovations could be centralized and provide transferrable knowledge.

While the initial plan was just demonstration farms, this was eventually linked into a larger initiative within ITC to launch a horticulture program, targeting both processed and fresh fruits and vegetables for the local and export markets.

New Engagement Model

The demonstration farms would showcase improved production and harvesting techniques (e.g. irrigation, plant beds, intercropping, greenhouses), and new crop varieties, and eventually provide links to new markets for improved crops. The farms would demonstrate a menu of options, ranging from tying up tomato plants to installing a greenhouse, so farmers could choose which techniques they wanted to adopt. ITC had four main goals for the demonstration plot program: 1) increasing quantity; 2) improving quality; 3) reducing costs; and 4) diversifying crops. The goal was for each farmer to grow at least a quarter of an acre of new crop varieties.

The pilot included six one-acre plots and one 27-acre installation for more intensive training. All pilots were located in the state of Madhya Pradesh. At each plot, a nursery sold high-quality seedlings, a key element of improving production. Five categories of crops were shown at each plot: (1) horticulture/high value; (2) organics; (3) aromatic and medicinal plants; (4) regular/traditional; and (5) Indian spices. In total, the plots showcased 350 crop varieties.

ITC built off its successful Sanchalak network to disseminate best practices and publicize the activities of the demonstration farms. ITC agents were posted in each of the pilot villages to provide day-to-day agricultural advice. They identified progressive farmers in each community to serve as lead farmers to showcase techniques to the village. To scale up the program, ITC would use a train-the-trainers approach, hiring farmers to work on the demonstration plots who could then serve as trainers for their communities. ITC would maintain overall management of the program, estimating demand for each crop and managing supply so the market was not flooded with a crop when there was only limited demand.

Through its demonstration plots, ITC was building a network of global resource partners who had been critical participants since the inception phase of the program. The main partners for this activity were:

1. *Nunhems*, a seed producing company, supplied the hybrid seeds to sell through the ITC channel. Its product offerings were the most appropriate for the Indian agro-climate, and it had invested significant resources in research and development for new varieties.
2. *Bayer*, a German company, brought years of experience in crop science and assisted with best practices, fertilizers, and pesticides.
3. *International Development Enterprises India* was the partner for drip irrigation technologies.
4. *Well Grow*, an internal ITC department, supplied neem-based organic fertilizers.
5. *The Central Institute for Medicinal and Aromatic Plants* provided best practices for the medicinal and aromatic category.
6. *Agriculture universities* brought agricultural expertise and research knowledge.

Once the pilot was completed and the business model perfected, ITC planned to reach out to government and local extension agents as additional partners.

Preliminary Results

ITC witnessed some initial success with its demonstration plots:

> Omkar Singh Sahu visited the ITC demonstration plot to learn about approved techniques and chose to adopt a few new practices for his tomatoes. He applied fertilizer and pesticides, purchased improved seedlings, and put his tomato plants into stalks. With these techniques, he saw a five-fold increase in the price per kilo he received for his tomatoes, with expenses of only 8,500 rupees. Based on his success, other farmers visited his farm to learn about the new techniques, and he was considering investing in drip irrigation.

Dhasi Dheriya was inspired by visiting Sahu's farm and purchased improved seeds, and created crop beds for his eggplant. When his farm became too wet, he was advised to tie up his plants, but chose not to make the investment. Unfortunately his eggplants became too wet and rotted, confirming for him the importance of stalking his plants in the future.

Harirampal already had a diversified farm, with marigolds, tomatoes, eggplant, potatoes and okra. After talking with an ITC village representative, he decided to stalk his tomatoes and create beds for his crops. He readily saw his crops appear healthier.

Employment Exchange

During the strategic discussions for e-Choupal 3.0 it became obvious that not only did ITC need to diversify, but the farmers did too. Agricultural land holdings per person were decreasing and it was becoming more and more difficult to support a family on agriculture alone. In the e-Choupal areas, 5% of 21 to 30-year-olds were unemployed graduates, and 90% of them were looking for job opportunities outside agriculture.[5] Many wanted to stay in their local area, but had difficulty finding job opportunities. Complementary sources of income were desperately needed. Demand for employees in the rural areas was also increasing. With increasing rural expansion, businesses needed front-line employees in tier 1, 2, and 3 cities, but it was very expensive and time-consuming to recruit qualified candidates. There were job providers and qualified candidates, but no way to match them up. With ITC's rural network already established through the Sanchalaks, there was a clear opportunity for ITC to serve as the link between job seekers and hiring companies.

New Engagement Model

The employment exchange was intended to be a one-stop portal to exchange job openings, training opportunities, and career advice. Created in partnership with Monster.com, the portal was being developed to provide job postings and networking opportunities much like similar sites in the United States and Europe.

While the employment portal would be accessible from any computer, the access point would be through Sanchalaks. The Sanchalak would play an essential role, verifying the identity of the job applicant to provide traceability through the system. Employers demanded traceability and integrity, and the Sanchalaks provided an existing link into rural communities. To minimize opportunities for corruption, the Sanchalak would have no involvement after identity verification and no impact over the employment decision. If the applicant received an offer letter, the Sanchalak would receive a commission. ITC and other portal partners would receive ad revenue and transaction fees.

ITC e-Choupal 3.0 Enablers

The complexity of the new businesses conceived within e-Choupal 3.0 required a strong foundation of enablers to support these new anchor businesses and deeper personalization efforts. The horizontal enablers that applied to all the pillars (new businesses) fell into three overarching categories: technology, convergence, and social architecture.

Technology

Technology had been the crux of enabling the e-Choupal network from 1.0 through the expansion to 2.0. Underpinning this complex business model was a complex Enterprise Resource Planning system that enabled Choupal Saagars to manage their daily demand and inflow of different agricultural commodities from farmers, and helped determine each day's buying price.

As ITC's e-Choupal model expanded across India, ITC recognized the opportunity for deeper, broader, and more personalized expansion through mobile technology, including capturing data from farmers about their soil, crops, and overall needs. This would create base for analytics to anticipate and develop solutions for farmers. In part this would be done by partnering with other multi-national companies and providing them the data collected from farmers. Mobile technology would achieve both personalization and the opportunity to scale the solution in a more cost-effective manner.

To develop this model, ITC partnered with Nokia to think about how to personalize what each farmer received, and how to develop a user-friendly interface that would secure farmer adoption of using mobile technology for transactions previously conducted through the e-Choupal computer. One critical point of feedback that emerged through the co-creation process with farmers was the need for customization by language (Hindi, Tamil, etc.).

One of the lessons ITC learned from e-Choupal 1.0 was that adoption was quicker when the value creation opportunity was clearer to the farmers. This was based on the premise that people's intuitive ability to use technology is very different if they understand and appreciate the value from the use of new technology. Therefore, ITC first focused on demonstrating the value of the mobile business model, and then rolled out the mobile technology platform.

As ITC's e-Choupal model continued to scale, it was becoming increasingly difficult for ITC staff to interact with farmers individually to serve them with customized solutions and advice. Interactions between farmers and ITC staff became intermittent in some areas, as ITC's staff was stretched to serve more and more farmers. So a benefit of mobile phone technology was to provide farmers with a vehicle to communicate their needs and requests (for questions on the health of a crop, or to order certain agri-inputs, or even to send in questions through SMS text messaging). A secondary benefit was the ability to receive information on one's mobile phone in real time, without the need to go to the Sanchalak's home to use the e-Choupal computer.

For example, a farmer could send in a digital picture of a diseased crop taken with the mobile phone to obtain advice on what to do to fix it. The value for ITC was in certain data that a farmer could input into a mobile phone that would greatly help ITC better understand the agricultural landscape of India by different soil regions so as to better manage what ITC advised different farmers to grow in different areas of the land, and what ITC could advise its partner companies to develop based on the needs of these farmers.

Another use of mobile technology was to support the FMCG deeper personalization effort. It had been challenging to obtain information on the commercial exchange between village retailers and their consumers. Therefore, ITC had not been able to formally capture any consumer insights that could help it penetrate the rural market more effectively. So ITC explored using mobile technology to create the smart exchange described within the FMCG section (above). The purpose was to allow retailers to order directly from the Samyojak or distribution center, thus enabling smart decision-making by ITC to sell and even develop new products to meet demand in the villages. At the heart of this model was enabling personalization for ordering and distribution service for the retailers through a connected resource. This provided retailers with the opportunity to also access partner companies that were leveraging this channel to connect to retailers and consumers in rural India. Younger retailers seemed to be receptive to the idea and saw the value of ordering goods through their mobile phone.

The areas in scope were to use mobile technology for obtaining and delivering information to and from farmers, and for FMCG order fulfillment and tracking. At a future point, once the rural employment new anchor business was launched, it might also be supported with the mobile technology platform.

Mobile Business Model

One of the challenges facing ITC in deploying the mobile platform was determining who should pay for the farmer's mobile communication. ITC needed to think about the draw for the farmers to feed in the data, particularly if they had to spend their own money to send this information via text messaging.

One of the models under consideration was for ITC to charge agri-input partner companies for the data. Agri-input forecasting was very difficult in India, and the mobile data from the farmers would be particularly beneficial for agri-input companies to forecast demand. Thus, ITC believed farm input companies would be willing to pay for the data farmers provided. One way this could work was for ITC to pay farmers to input data based on what the agri-input dealers were willing to pay to obtain the data. Technically, this would be user-built content, wherein the farmer provided information that sat in a data repository and then could be sold to ITC partners.

Another option was for ITC to send market information to farmers through cell phones. The information would still be free, but mobile transmission costs would exist (for mobile phone costs or web browsing). Because farmers could receive this information for free from the e-Choupal on the computer, ITC was skeptical that farmers would pay for this information on their phones, particularly small farmers with low margins.

ITC believed three kinds of revenue models were possible:

1. User pays for part of what is received: The farmer would pay for the information (but only a small portion of actual cost). The value of charging the user would be in making ITC more accountable when users had to purchase information. For instance, there could be an expected service level agreement for ITC to send responses to farmers' questions within a given turnaround time.
2. Integrate user into the value chain and find ways to capture value there: ITC and partners could extract value from the information the farmers provided by using that info to penetrate the market more effectively. Increased revenues would pay for the cost of the technology.
3. Create an exchange: Because many people wanted to sell and buy, ITC could explore incentive structures within the value chain of matching up different value chain players. For instance, with FMCG linking retailers to sourcing of goods, and Sanchalaks for distribution of the goods, the Sanchalak would have a greater incentive to make the transactions occur, since the Sanchalak made commissions on the goods.

ITC's intended mobile platform would enable personalized solutions for the businesses that were part of 3.0 (FMCG, agri-inputs and demo plots, and employment). ITC's use of mobile technology for 3.0 demonstrated the concepts of deeper personalization, enabling wider access to resources, and the power of analytics to map a whole country's agriculture landscape and drive its agricultural productivity with customized agri-inputs.

Information and Communication Technology Architecture

The business models of ITC e-Choupal in the three phases discussed in this case were all supported by the underlying information and communication technology architecture. As noted earlier in the case, in the initial conceptualization of the e-Choupal idea, senior leadership at ITC chose technology as a means to achieve rural connectivity and eliminate information asymmetry. As result, the capabilities in their technology architecture were viewed as critical in their ability to execute their strategy and vision. In this section we track the evolution of the information and communication technology architecture that shaped and supported the respective stages of business model evolution.

Technology in e-Choupal 1.0

In version 1.0 (started in June 2000), the business goal was to create a physical infrastructure of e-Choupals at the village level and create community ownership of the initiative through the identified Sanchalaks. The main business objective here was to remove the information asymmetry in the supply chain, improve operational efficiency and enhance the farmer's experience in the process. At this stage an important technical challenge was creating a local language portal, which provided the required information to farmers such as local weather, market prices, and best practices, and supported the business goal.

Some of the other technology challenges in this phase were:

- Managing environmental aspects such as positioning computer and other equipment in villages and enabling connectivity
- Imparting skills to first-time Internet users in remote areas of rural India
- Personalization of content for the very fragmented and heterogeneous farmer groups; there was a separate website for each of the crop and language combinations (e.g., soyachoupal for soya beans, aquachoupal for marine products, plantersnet for coffee)

However, these features and functionality were not readily available off the shelf and had to be developed or tweaked in-house. For example, in order to support local language, the use of ActiveX controls for local language display purpose meant that the same had to be downloaded to the user's machine (i.e. Sanchalak's machine in the village). This took a long time in areas where the connectivity was poor. Hence an alternative approach was adopted. A simple text control attached to a local font was developed in-house. This led to faster download and display of dynamic contents. The fonts were developed in-house in certain cases to get a better visual effect.

The connectivity infrastructure was primitive and required massive effort and investments to make it fit for use in e-Choupal context. With the help of telecom companies, the connectivity infrastructure was upgraded. The ITC team also customized content and optimized the web pages for faster download under the limited bandwidth available. For example, images were optimized with special techniques, static contents in the web pages were cached in local machines, and dynamic content pages were developed with a template-driven approach for faster access.

The e-Choupal Version 1.0 technology goals were significantly influenced by the need to create access infrastructure, its availability, local language content, and information publishing. Basic analytics based on identity capture of the farmer, quality of produce, and price trends in various markets were facilitated through the information systems. The integration layers among farm, village, hub, and back office were still intermediated through manual and batch systems.

Technology in e-Choupal 2.0

In e-Choupal 2.0 (started in August 2004) the business model shifted from viewing farmers only as suppliers to seeing them as consumers as well. Hence new lines of business and services streams got added to the business model. The intent then changed to get the farmer and the retail outlets registered and transacting by selling directly from the village. This goal required creation of a flexible transaction portal, which integrated directly to the back-end ERP and ensured that there was no latency in processing any of the transactions.

The individual websites (soyachoupal, aquachoupal, etc.) were all integrated into one single portal (www.echoupal.com) for umbrella branding and consistent user experience. It facilitated an integrated view of business operations as the agri-commodities procurement crossed over to several states (e.g. soya beans procurement started in Maharashtra and Karnataka). It also facilitated a seamless coordination of rural distribution business by providing control of inventory.

ITC adopted a flexible business process platform and content management architecture to manage multiple web-fronts (crop, language, state combinations) through a single content engine and publishing system. Filtering features provided ability to select content relevant to the season, crop, and region. This architecture enabled a variety of business processes from multiple partners of ITC, including tractor manufacturers, insurance firms, aqua product companies, and others. In addition to supporting the evolving nature of these businesses, this architecture allowed business processes to be easily modified.

In addition, everything moved to Unicode-based language fonts to manage the local language requirements. This reduced maintenance overheads involved in customized fonts and made it easier for anyone to plug in and start using the e-Choupal facilities without having to go through a painful set-up process.

The back-end ERP systems were integrated with the front-end business process and transaction portal for seamless integration that facilitated order capture, quality, and customer data. The information started becoming more real-time, and improved visibility and control over the supply chain—both on the incoming agri-commodity procurement channel and the outward-bound rural distribution channel. Planning models and analytical tools helped in better territory coverage, outlet coverage, and forecast estimations, besides maximizing cross-selling opportunities with the same customer. The connectivity infrastructure was upgraded too—e-Choupals were connected through broadband VSATs that enabled always-on connectivity and fast Internet access.

Technology in e-Choupal 3.0

In e-Choupal 3.0 (started in April 2009), the business goal was to create a personalized co-creation platform to support a full-fledged "meta market." The meta market would enable operators such as input providers and rural distributors to create and exchange value using the e-Choupal platform. The participants included micro-entreprenuers in the village, farmers, rural youth, product manufacturers, services providers, and employers. The strategic intent was for all these people to plug into the network, collaborate, and transact through integrated systems on a pan-India scale.

A secure and comprehensive farmers-rural outlets-consumers database with all information pertaining to their holdings, consumption preferences, family details, and credit-worthiness, was being built to bring the personalization scope to an individual level. This database was the pivot around which the new services and products would be developed and offered. This information was expected to facilitate co-creation opportunities and engagement with the individual, to enable unique customer experience.

The access infrastructure was also undergoing revolutionary change through mobile telecom technology. This shift to the mobile platform was a must to achieve personalization. It meant that villagers could access services at any time and removed the dependence on a fixed-location infrastructure at a Sanchalak's house.

As the network expanded, the security and integrity of the systems was of paramount importance. Besides a firewall and intrusion detection systems, the RSA security token technology was in the process of being woven into the website to provide a comprehensive authentication and access mechanism.

In summary, the technology architecture would revolve around an integrated multi-commodity, multi-product, multi-service, and multi-language rural exchange with physical delivery and customer service delivered through network partners. The network would be real-time, accessible from anywhere, with fine slivers of personalization features and the ability to slice and dice the information for emerging patterns of needs and requirements of the participants. The technical capabilities and business model evolution at ITC were not independent. Information technology was the backbone supporting the complexity of all of ITC's e-Choupal businesses. ITC's e-Choupal from the onset had been built upon a scalable component-based architecture that enabled the ITC technical team to easily build upon the base architecture in designing the 3.0 prototype. Technology would be the backbone to deliver the value proposition and enable personalization and smart exchange. The security management of ITC's base information technology was very strong. This was particularly useful as the technical team built provisions for security of data transmission through the mobile interface.

Convergence

The e-Choupal, since its initial launch as part of 1.0, had been considered a convergence point that enabled informed choices and knowledge exchanges regarding transactions. ITC saw great potential in tapping into this natural tendency for social convergence around the e-Choupal. However, as the e-Choupal initiative expanded across India, and Sanchalaks were limited, ITC looked to find efficient economies of scale. Tapping into convergence as a platform enabler, therefore, became critical for further expansion. Additionally, there was a general recognition that it was really only the farmers who converged around the e-Choupal at the Sanchalak's house. ITC recognized the need to find or create additional locations for convergence points where people could engage and make informed choices.

New Model

ITC wanted to expand on enabling convergence points for social networking, both physically and virtually, to support communities in their expression of needs, and to engage members of the community, such as women, who had not yet been engaged in the e-Choupal model. One way ITC was attempting to foster greater convergence points was in physical spaces, such as at village Haats (a physical meeting place) as well as Haats in cities where rural artisans came together (for example, Dilli Haat in New Delhi). Another means of convergence being explored was in virtual spaces over the Internet. ITC referred to this latter concept as virtual Addas, which means third place, considered a place other than home and work—a third place where people liked to naturally converge, be it at coffee shops, malls, tea or paan stalls, or other such points of convergence that draw people for social networking. ITC hoped to tap into this concept to foster greater social networking both in physical spaces and through the Internet, and leverage these points of convergence for dissemination of information and services, as well as listening points to gather feedback on what consumers desired and needed. At a later point, ITC planned to move the virtual Adda to the mobile platform.

The first step of the pilot prototype was to understand the dynamics of the convergence points. Based on a thorough analysis of physical, virtual, natural, and engineered congregation points, the ITC management team tried to tease out the key insights by observing the drivers for convergence and opportunities that remained to be untapped at such points. Across examples from the Paan Bhandar (a small shop) to malls to coffee shops (namely Café Coffee Day), parks, bus stands, and Internet-based convergence points such as Facebook, eBay, and Sunsilk Gang of Girls, ITC discovered the draw of a third or neutral place where people tend to converge for an experience to get away and take a break. The analysis revealed key opportunity insights for ITC to act upon, namely the types of services ITC could market and the partnerships it could establish in existing ecosystems. ITC was particularly keen to understand this so as to not disturb the social fabric of an existing social ecosystem when introducing services.

The business objective of the convergence points was to provide a space for people to make informed decisions about services available to them through natural, physical, and online channels. Rural Haats were considered one such natural convergence point. ITC was interested in leveraging the existing traffic going to a rural Haat by offering a set of relevant (noncompetitive) products and services to the rural consumer. The point was to spread awareness, build excitement, generate leads and aggregate demand for ITC products and services. **Figure 7** shows the different basket of offerings intended to be shared at such convergence points.

The first ITC convergence pilot occurred at a Haat on December 21, 2008, in a village called Hardoi (a three-hour drive from the city of Lucknow). The point of this pilot was to co-create a convergence experience from the ground up with the Sanchalak, and to demonstrate the value proposition to the Sanchalak in marketing various ITC and partner services and products to the people selling and buying at the Hardoi Haat. Convergence points such as the Hardoi Haat tended to attract around 2,000 people who came in from around 15 villages twice a week. Goods sold at this Haat ranged from the most popular items of food grains, vegetables, fruits, and spices to teas, snacks, clothes, hair accessories, and other miscellaneous items, including bicycle parts and repair services.

Figure 7

Basket of Offerings at Convergence Points

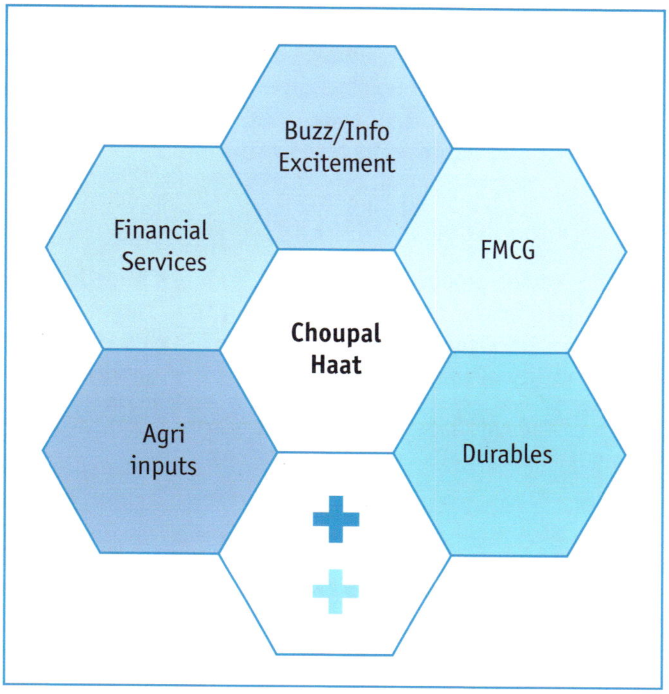

ITC had set up a stall offering an assortment of ITC FMCG products and a range of partner services including life insurance (through partnership with Life Insurance Corporation of India), general Insurance (motor, health), and credit card services (through partnership with SBI). Additionally, ITC's partner John Deere was there advertising its products and services, including a tractor on display. ITC's partners had found it difficult to penetrate rural markets and therefore partnered with ITC to promote awareness of their products and services at such convergence points. At this first pilot, ITC and its partners ran promotions to draw in foot traffic. For instance, ITC ran a promotion through a dart board game, where each person was charged one rupee for three throws. Anyone who succeeded in hitting the bull's-eye won one ITC soap. John Deere ran a promotion where it offered free maintenance and service for the first ten tractors it sold. The stall also offered free basic medical check-ups.

The overall effort of using the Haat as a convergence point appeared to be promising, particularly in drawing people from the community who were not farmers and had not yet been as exposed to such products and services. The Sanchalak was to be instrumental in the success of this platform, both in providing ITC credibility to his community as well as in communicating feedback from the community to ITC in what the community really liked and wanted more of versus services that the community did not see value in. ITC hoped to use such convergence points as a platform to draw further insights for personalization of products and services. **Table 1** outlines the role ITC expected each stakeholder to play in the process and the respective value proposition drawing each group into the convergence model.

Table 1

Stakeholder	Role/Responsibility	Value Proposition
ITC-Agribusiness Division	Concept and communication design, initial implementation, bringing in partner companies, working out revenue models	• Awareness spread • Lead generation • Subsequent conversions
Sanchalak	Word of mouth propaganda, anchoring the Choupal Haat	• Increased earnings from sales
Partner Companies	Provide product/service/ information/promotional support to enhance the functional/aesthetic utility of the Choupal Haat	• Directly connect with target audience • Platform for promotion of products and subsequent sales
Local independent entrepreneurs (Vet, GP, eetc.)	Augment all above services to drive more footfalls to the Choupal Haat	• Direct revenue

Social Architecture

The third enabler was the reorganization of the social architecture that was critical for the successful deployment of the new businesses. ITC attempted to reorganize the social architecture by working with Sanchalaks to facilitate community pull and working with the ITC hub teams to drive the back-end.

Original Model

An ITC hub was a buying center of the agricultural commodities and the rural distribution of FMCG. In addition, financial services and agri-inputs were coordinated through the hub. The hub was primarily driven by sourcing targets, rural distribution targets, and financial services targets. The hub pushed down the business targets to the Sanchalak, who was an extended arm of ITC in the village.

Over time, Sanchalaks had been losing interest due to the gap between the initial aspirations and perceived effort and realized earnings. Some Sanchalaks started off very well, but underperformed later, while others were never very engaged. The hub teams were pushing the Sanchalaks and Samyojaks, managing the environment, and reporting to the ITC branch office, and had no time or energy to work with the Sanchalaks to re-engage them, which led to a feeling of helplessness. The hub teams justified the lack of engagement by saying that the Sanchalaks were not interested or capable, the Samyojaks were not cooperative, the village potential was limited, or that the branch was asking for too many reports. At the end of the day, these stakeholders were tired and not always happy with the achievements.

These feelings came from many sources. For the Sanchalaks, there were some limitations due to the social dynamics, as the Sanchalak could not reach out to all the communities in the villages, because of social hierarchy or gender considerations. One of the main ideas behind ITC's e-Choupal initiative was to empower the villages by providing them with information so that they could transact with better bargaining power. But the information and transaction were concentrated with one person in the village—the Sanchalak. There was a need to unbundle this, because ITC was not able to reach out to the entire community without excluding certain segments due to the limitations of the Sanchalak.

ITC wanted to play a relevant role in the rural communities. For the company's offerings to be customized to the village, the hub interface had to have the capacity to not only maintain the existing services, such as procurement and distribution, but also to start engaging with the village community and the Sanchalak in a personalized manner to understand what could be customized. There were many income-generating opportunities inside the village, if ITC could leverage what was already happening in the rural communities. The hub could understand what else the village needed, either through having a method to decode how the village talks or by interacting with the Sanchalak, and be the node to feed the information and ideas back to the ITC network. The company could use these insights to collaborate with partner companies. These partners could start to pick up the understanding of what the ecosystem needed and offer new products or services, which could be distributed through ITC. To enable this, the role of the hub would have to shift from being an administrative outpost to an entrepreneurial thinking entity that desired to grow its own catchment area independently.

New Engagement Model

The social architecture was a horizontal enabler of all the existing businesses and new businesses ITC planned to initiate. The framework within which the company had established its presence was changing, and if the company wanted to create a more enabled and, therefore, more open ecosystem for rapid deployment, development, and innovation, the social architecture needed to change. Instead of an administrative approach, an entrepreneurial approach would be required. Apart from executing the existing business of commodity procurement and rural distribution, an entrepreneurial hub would enhance the existing core revenue proposition by building relationships with the village, Sanchalaks and service providers to deliver enhanced services. The entrepreneurial hub would identify new opportunities for growth by intercepting, capturing, collating, and reporting emerging trends, tastes, and business propositions in the hub ecosystem and co-create new possibilities.

The Sanchalak provided a critical link to engage with the village and therefore was crucial to this engagement. As part of 3.0, ITC planned to try to profile Sanchalaks on different parameters such as the village potential, the Sanchalak's skills, and the resources and ability to deliver the value propositions. For example, selling insurance is very different from selling FMCG. While rural distribution of FMCG was very tangible, selling insurance, which is a deferred benefit that is uncertain, required the Sanchalak to be able to think conceptually and communicate the benefits to the customers. ITC aimed to assess the Sanchalak on the basis of his suitability for each kind of business and understand his preference for engaging in different businesses.

Sanchalaks are historically successful farmers, but if ITC wanted them to do many other things, the company needed to better understand their attitudes and aptitudes. It became essential to know what motivated Sanchalaks and identify the skills required to perform the role. Sanchalaks had different motivations. For some, there was an innate need to develop an alternate source of income; others who did not understand the business preferred to wait and watch. Every Sanchalak engaged differently and a one-size-fits-all engagement, which worked very well for the procurement-led business, was not going to work for e-Choupal 3.0. Different types of communication approaches were needed for different Sanchalaks.

ITC had a lot of data about the villages where it had a presence and was planning to analyze that data to come up with a diagnosis. Based on some parameters, the company wanted to be able to classify the village and determine which villages required certain kinds of services. This would help in devising a tool kit for the hub so that it could become an entrepreneurial hub.

Village progress indicators were very key elements to understanding how people in a particular village measured success, growth, and development. They could differ from village to village. It was important to understand the villages' desire for growth, how growth happened and what was critical for the village to grow. ITC wanted the hub to be able to interpret the needs of development in a manner that would translate into a particular service. In some cases this could be an employment exchange and in others it could be education and training. The services and solutions had to be what the village needed rather than what ITC believed would be good for that particular village. Earlier, hubs used to get business targets. Under the new plan they would identify opportunities.

Conclusion

ITC has come a long way in positively impacting the lives of farmers across India through its e-Choupal initiative. From e-Choupal 1.0 to 2.0 to the formation of 3.0, ITC has demonstrated tremendous dedication to learning from each of its implementations and addressing key issues and opportunities. Most importantly, ITC has been instrumental in building a foundation for sustainable commercial engagement in rural India, viewing the challenges in the rural supply chain as business opportunities, and pioneering rural commerce for the base of the pyramid. Of greatest significance was ITC's ability to meet both its profit and social impact goals by structuring the e-Choupal initiative as a win-win deal for ITC and Indian farmers as both micro-producers and micro-consumers. The beauty of the business model was that ITC's profits were predicated on factors that carried huge social benefits.

ITC aimed to go a step further with e-Choupal 3.0 in tapping into the innovative mindset of farmers by co-creating with farmers as micro-entrepreneurs. How effective ITC would continue to be with its implementation of 3.0 would probably not be seen until 2011, and the benefits might only start to be visible even later.

What challenges will ITC face in implementing 3.0? What changes should it consider to the structure described above, and are there components and services they should add? Imagine what the Indian agricultural landscape will look like, particularly at the base of the pyramid, once ITC co-creates personalized solutions with farmers. Based on this future, what will e-Choupal 4.0 look like and what should CEO Sivakumar consider about the future of this project?

Endnotes

[1] Prahalad, C.K. *The Fortune at the Bottom of the Pyramid: Eradicating Poverty Through Profits*. Wharton School Publishing. 2006.

[2] Anupindi, Ravi and Sivakumar, S. "ITC's e-Choupal: A Platform Strategy for Rural Transformation," Presentation, December 2005

[3] Prahalad, C.K. *The Fortune at the Bottom of the Pyramid: Eradicating Poverty Through Profits*. Wharton School Publishing. 2006.

[4] Anupindi, Ravi and Sivakumar, S. "ITC's e-Choupal: A Platform Strategy for Rural Transformation," Presentation, December 2005

[5] ITC presentation

Notes

Made in the USA
Las Vegas, NV
07 November 2026

57672681R00017